Tell Us How to Live

Ace Boggess

Fernwood
PRESS

Tell Us How to Live

©2025 by Ace Boggess

Fernwood Press
Newberg, Oregon
www.fernwoodpress.com

All rights reserved. No part may be reproduced
for any commercial purpose by any method without
permission in writing from the copyright holder.

Printed in the United States of America

Cover and page design: Eric Muhr
Cover photo: davide ragusa on Unsplash
Author photo: Grace Welch

ISBN 978-1-59498-174-6

Ace Boggess's brilliantly original book consists entirely of poems with interrogative titles and unexpected responses in verse. It is not merely a collection but a unified book. The first question is, "Do You Have Any Advice for Inmates?" Boggess has the right to answer because he has done time. In one poem, he describes himself as an "unemployed ex-con hiding in a red state" (he also has a law degree). These are real poems, not the products of some enlightened prison workshop. With wit and a wonderful speed of association, Boggess addresses such subjects as luck, loss, music, adultery, drugs, and guns, with references, sometimes surprising, to Hamlet, the Serenity prayer, the Divine, Van Morrison, "the Schopenhauer of punk," and Don Giovanni, among other cultural landmarks. The book has charm and humor, and it is also deeply moving: "You'd like to be / the hero once, but it's you who walked through gates / afraid, as though you've been on trial all your life."

—DAVID LEHMAN
series editor, *Best American Poetry*
author of *The Evening Sun* and *The Morning Line*

Ace Boggess's *Tell Us How to Live* is a thrilling inquiry into lived experiences and the nature of observation, rendered through an innovative and intriguing premise. In this book, haunting poems portray the haunted, inspirations spin out into further implications, and etymology and exploration reign. "You have to feed the memory," Boggess writes, and in doing so, he feeds the reader's spirit, too. The structure of the book is particularly inviting, as each title poses a question and premise so that, as a reader, one feels in intimate conversation with the vast pantheon of figures and documents that provide them, as well as with Boggess himself. These queries are charged with urgency, humor, and pathos, and in response, Boggess nimbly shifts between forms, voices, and concepts to craft poems that are sensitive, clever, and poignant in turn. What results is a tribute to the human spirit and a triumph of a collection.

—KENZIE ALLEN
author of *Cloud Missives*

Ace Boggess's *Tell Us How to Live* is pure delight. I love how every poem's title is a quotation, whether it be from Shakespeare, a Facebook post, Socrates, a rehab workbook, Goodreads, Whitman, or Dostoevsky. I relish this book for its luminous foray into the speaker's psyche and for revelatory lines like "Find happiness as often as you can & / hold it to your lips like chocolate" and "There's too much human / in being human, & not enough / being." Providing just the right blend of humor and wisdom, Boggess has created the perfect book for getting us through the toughest of times.

—MARTHA SILANO
author of *Gravity Assist*
and *This One We Call Ours*

for Randi Ward and Andrea Fekete,
good friends and writers,

and, of course, for Grace Welch
with love and answers

Contents

Other Books by This Author 11
Acknowledgments 13
I. 17
"Do You Have Any Advice for Inmates?" 19
"Could This Be Where I Premiere My Memories?" 20
"How Would You Rate Your Wellness?" 21
"What Feelings Did You Try to Manage?" 22
"Has It Gotten Easier to Avoid Drugs as You've Gotten
   Older?" 23
"Prefer Slick, Feverish Grooves Over Funky Backbeats?" 24
"What Is Your Favorite Movie?" 26
"Are Your Emotions More or Less Intense?" 28
"Is Not That Which Is Loved in Some State Either of
   Becoming or Suffering?" 29
"Are You Worried About a Breakdown?" 30
"Does That Mean You Really Want Me to Have a Terrible
   Day?" 31
"Do You Think of Yourself as a Winner?" 32

"What Makes You Happy?" 33

II. 35
"Who Am I That I Am Not on Trial or in Prison?" 37
"So What Is the Line Between Memory and Hallucination?" 38
"Isn't It Gravity That Ultimately Gives the Grave
   Its Gravitas?" 39
"If I Came in Here Shot, Would You Say I Had a
   Lead Problem?" 40
"What Is Your Idle Job?" 42
"Can Cockroaches Die of a Broken Heart?" 43
"Would You Be Willing to Bail Me Out?" 44
"Then Why Am I Made with Such Desires?" 45
"What Have You Lost?" 46
"Have You Ever Loved Someone and Still Felt Lonely?" 48
"What Will You Do If You Hit the Jackpot?" 49
"It's a Sexual Song, Isn't It, That Crickets Sing?" 50
"Did You Ever Switch from One Drug to Another?" 51
"How Do I Get a Signed Copy?" 52
"Would Any of Your Friends Enjoy Adultery?" 53
"Shall I Send You Some Bitter Broth?" 54
"But What Are You Celebrating?" 55
"Do You Like Yourself?" 56
"Isn't Today Worth Fighting For?" 57
"Why Are There So Many Starlings, Darling?" 58
"Where Do You Go Between Breaths?" 60
"Do You Think It'll Be Okay?" 61

III. 63
"Couldn't I Tell Them Other Truths?" 65
"What Syllable Do I Chant for God to Hear Me, and at
   What Frequency?" 66
"Can You Really Get By on Three Chords and the Truth?" ... 67
"Don't You Know That Night Is Coming?" 68
"Have You Thought About Your Funeral?" 69

"What Do You Most Want People to Say About You When You're Gone?" 70
"Why Do I Have to Die?" 71
"Why Is America So Obsessed with Guns?" 72
"Why Don't You Wear a Watch?" 73
"Do You Hear the Wind Rising All Around You?" 74
"Moreover, What on the Face of the Earth Could Have the Slightest Value for Me?" 76
"I Want to Be a Minor Poet, but Does That Mean I Have to Be Sad All the Time?" 77
"Who Do You Love If Not Yourself?" 78
"How's Life Out There in the Real World?" 79
"So, When Do You Want to Die?" 80
"But Won't You Tell Us How to Live?" 81

Title Index 83
First Line Index 87
About the Author 91

Other Books by This Author

Poetry
- My Pandemic / Gratitude List
- Escape Envy
- Misadventure
- I Have Lost the Art of Dreaming It So
- Ultra Deep Field
- The Prisoners
- The Beautiful Girl Whose Wish Was Not Fulfilled

Novels
- States or Mercy
- A Song Without a Melody

Short Stories
- Always One Mistake

Acknowledgments

The author wishes to thank the following publications in which these poems first appeared, often in different forms:

Antietam Review: "Don't You Know That Night Is Coming?"
Another Chicago Magazine: "Why Don't You Wear a Watch?"
Apeiron Review: "Why Is America So Obsessed with Guns?"
As It Ought to Be: "Are Your Emotions More or Less Intense?"
Atticus Review: "Could This Be Where I Premiere My Memories?"
Bellingham Review: "What Feelings Did You Try to Manage?"
Blood Orange Review: "Is Not That Which Is Loved in Some State Either of Becoming or Suffering?"
The Bryant Literary Review: "Prefer Slick, Feverish Grooves Over Funky Backbeats?"
Chiron Review: "What Do You Most Want People to Say About You When You're Gone?" and "Has It Gotten Easier to Avoid Drugs as You've Gotten Older?"
Cider Press Review: "Does That Mean You Really Want Me to Have a Terrible Day?"
Clackamas Literary Review: "What Syllable Do I Chant for God to Hear Me, and at What Frequency?"

Concho River Review: "How Do I Get a Signed Copy?"
Connecticut River Review: "Shall I Send You Some Bitter Broth?"
Constellations: "Why Are There So Many Starlings, Darling?"
Crab Orchard Review: "What Will You Do If You Hit the Jackpot?"
Dream Pop Journal: "What Makes You Happy?"
Dunes Review: "Do You Think of Yourself as a Winner?"
The Indianapolis Review: "What Have You Lost?"
Jabberwock Review: "Then Why Am I Made with Such Desires?"
Jenny: "Can You Really Get By on Three Chords and the Truth?"
Kestrel: "But Won't You Tell Us How to Live?" and "Couldn't I Tell Them Other Truths?"
The Manhattanville Review: "Are You Worried About a Breakdown?"
The Mantle: "Isn't Today Worth Fighting for?"
Michigan Quarterly Review: "How's Life Out There in the Real World?"
Muddy River Poetry Review: "Could Love Make You Sing Like That—Desperate, Terrible?"
Mud Season Review: "Have You Thought About Your Funeral?'
North Dakota Quarterly: "Who Am I That I Am Not on Trial or in Prison?"
Notre Dame Review: "Can Cockroaches Die of a Broken Heart?"
The Ocotillo Review: "How Would You Rate Your Wellness?"
Paris Lit Up: "Do You Hear the Wind Rising All Around You?"
Poetry East: "So What Is the Line Between Memory and Hallucination?" and "Who Do You Love If Not Yourself?"
RATTLE: "What Is Your Idle Job?"
Red Eft Review: "So, When Do You Want to Die?"
Red River Review: "Do You Like Yourself?"
River Heron Review: "I Want to Be a Minor Poet, but Does That Mean I Have to Be Sad All the Time?" and "Would You Be Willing to Bail Me Out?"
r.kv.r.y.: "Did You Ever Switch from One Drug to Another?"

Rockvale Review: "It's a Sexual Song, Isn't It, That Crickets Sing?"

Sheila-Na-Gig: "If I Came in Here Shot, Would You Say I Had a Lead Problem?" and "Where Do You Go Between Breaths?"

Soundings East: "Do You Have Any Advice for Inmates?"

South Carolina Review: "But What Are You Celebrating?"

Still: The Journal: "Have You Ever Loved Someone and Still Felt Lonely?"

Tar River Poetry: "Moreover, What on the Face of the Earth Could Have the Slightest Value for Me?"; "Isn't It Gravity That Ultimately Gives the Grave Its Gravitas?"; and "What Happened to the Twelfth Rose?"

Valparaiso Poetry Review: "What Is Your Favorite Movie?"

West Texas Literary Review: "Would Any of Your Friends Enjoy Adultery?" and "Why Do I Have to Die?"

West Trade Review: "Do You Think It'll Be Okay?"

"So What Is the Line Between Memory and Hallucination?" and "Prefer Slick, Feverish Grooves Over Funky Backbeats?" were reprinted in *Redux*. "Is Not That Which Is Loved in Some State Either of Becoming or Suffering?" was reprinted by *isacoustic*.

I.

"Do You Have Any Advice for Inmates?"

—Sarena Fox

Don't play Spades with your cellies at two in the morning
by jaundiced glow of the suicide light.
Results in *falling off your bunk* more than you'd like.

If you're passing a roll-up, don't get caught.
Facing the Magistrate, don't resist; say you did it,
tell a story or a joke, & ask him to be lenient.

Everyone has a different lesson
that must be learned by force, the hole, a broken bone.
Don't eat the fish. Don't snitch. Don't cheat

at cards or chess. Don't fall in love
with the cute C.O. who promises a secret spot,
unless you're doing life, & then why not?

How about this? Do laugh when possible,
then pass that on, rattling off one-liners
like having drinks with friends at the bar.

Find happiness as often as you can &
hold it to your lips like chocolate,
savor it like a new pillow, burn it into your flesh

like a tattoo you know you shouldn't get
but will because the blue enchants you &
the pain proves you're breathing after all.

"Could This Be Where I Premiere My Memories?"

—AceBot on what-would-i-say.com

The end of the year means now I begin
more recent stories, saying "This was back in X."
Perception of distance through the fabric-
cation of time. I'm standing in January like it's an airport,
glancing over my shoulder for home,
which I can't see, although it remained when I left it.
This time last year, I had a novel freshly minted &
girlfriend on suicide watch because her meds stopped working.
Pluses & minuses. I'm a poet again,
writing my history as if a castle I might explore
then leave to walk through bare gardens &
labyrinths of gray-dead oaks. Remember
last year when it was 70 degrees &
camellias pursed their candy-apple lips
in a world gone odd, in a culture of anger &
unanticipated violence? So long ago.
This month is about snow-blindness & Irish sweaters.
What seemed chaos has become routine
in the same way a prisoner, after years of confinement,
lives each day without noticing bars on the windows
of his cell. But that was further back than X for me, &
I've said enough about it. Let me focus
on my present past: fear of upcoming journeys
already caught in photographs, a few successes
raced beyond like mile markers, the words *It will be okay*
spoken too many times for comfort.
How did anyone survive it? Here we are.

"How Would You Rate Your Wellness?"

—medical questionnaire

It wouldn't win an Academy or National Book Award. Not enough weeping, though plenty of wounds flare in the heat, heart, hard enough to hurt like an accidental elbow to my eye. Some days my knee won't bend; others, it gives out on its own like a mug set carelessly on the counter's edge.

Back spasms, check. Out of shape beyond repair, check there, too. I'm ruined from artless savagery with food.

I'd give my wellness three stars out of five. I can (mostly) walk & (sometimes) fuck & (need be) run away from my own mistakes—nucleus of the problem, Dr. Healthcare Survey Writer.

That's the thing about which you never ask, as if mother believing the lie or father looking the other way. You ignore the flaw while questioning me, except when it comes to cigarettes: through this bold Helvetica, I recognize your condescending stare.

"What Feelings Did You Try to Manage?"

—rehab workbook

I almost blacked out reciting the tomorrow &
tomorrow & tomorrow speech
in my twelfth-grade English class:
panic-stricken, dizzied, pulse
stabbing at my neck (same way I felt
twenty years later, standing before the judge,
confessing what sordid prophets knew).
Not that I couldn't do it, didn't have it memorized,
failed to appreciate its sorrow—
like damp cardboard, I buckled, shaken
by anxieties I couldn't understand,
afraid of everyone watching.
I never handled other people well—
fear my tragic flaw leading to despair &
those three tomorrows: the tomorrow
of saying hello to strangers;
the tomorrow of putting on headphones
to drown me beneath fuzzy chords,
self-erasing; & the other one,
the tomorrow of desperate banquets &
my drug-dumb blade,
letting me not be me, not worry,
more Macbeth the plotter,
less the broken, weeping patron
waiting defiantly for the woods to burn.

"Has It Gotten Easier to Avoid Drugs as You've Gotten Older?"

—David Peyton

Avoid, yes. To want,
scars never vanish,
no lasering procedure
to erase them
like insensitive tattoos.

To want, dream of,
greedy is the body
with its need of touch
inside now like out.

Avoiding, I might hide
in my windowless room,
just me & my anxieties,
refusing the world a moment.

But want, God, want—
what would you save
from a house on fire?

When I visited
Carson McCullers's
childhood home,
a museum preserved as was,
I thought, out of habit,

Wonder if her family
left any pills
in the medicine cabinet, &
would they still be good
after all these years?

"Prefer Slick, Feverish Grooves Over Funky Backbeats?"

—TV advertisement

blessed rock'n'roll R & B funk folk acid jazz
blessed Beatles carnival barkers calling the modern era
blessed Doors Who Grateful Dead immortal
noodling licks on vinyl persistent as the low note
in my college neighbor's busy buzzing radiator
blessed Sam playing along
"there's a B-flat in my headboard"
blessed Joshua Redman
saxophone a second tongue whispering sweetest words in bed
blessed Rusted Root rhythmic re-animators of jam-band jam
blessing the crowd with dance shake mystery vibe
blessed locals Jeff Roy Tyler Kat Mike Speedy John Shawn
Annie leaving to return
savor diverse notes catchy refrains
heavy metal blaring
moaning blues
frayed like an old man's movement into night tonight
a Celtic quintet whistling bullets through
silk armor of a woman's voice
blessed Shenanigans classic Irish sweetness
melancholia groove & bounce
blessed Van Morrison soulful tone suffering slings & arrows
blessed techno Moby reggae Marley
ska la la da da de da de
blessed Freddie Mercury coy erotic reaching
"March of the Black Queen"
blessed sultry Shirley Manson "happy when it rains" &
sad to be in song blessed blessed blessed

pipers in the summer heat
center stage at Calamity Cafe
vanished-bar nostalgia welcome as the word 'welcome'
blessed release
in chords chorus tensing cadence
tribal as a movie about the white man's dream
of Africa
blessed background score to my climax falling action
end blessed end that hasn't found me yet
Sartre's silence punctuates a symphony
defines as much as first chords
solos arpeggios harmony
blue notes blessed blue notes &
violence in the interlude anticipating quiet
for the blessed listener's blessed blessed ear

"What Is Your Favorite Movie?"

—moviething.com

I lose myself in dialogue,
character caught in the opening rain.
I crave erotic moments
amidst London being shelled,
explosions from bombs & indignation.
I smell burning dust as I watch,
taste words that mean Goodbye-
I-love-you,
salty from tears & cooled by wine
(the unspoken words).
A friend told me once
the enduring (or eternal)
sorrow in Ralph Fiennes's eyes
reminded her what she saw in mine.
She meant Fiennes
in *The English Patient*,
not Greene's *End of the Affair*.
It's the same defeated character:
angry, alone & not,
smoldering with need
for another's wife.
Both men see their passion flare,
its kindling wane; both rage,
overwhelmed by man & the Divine.
One mourns in a wasteland of human hearts
where arid fury covers all details
with sand—lips dried from sunlight,
books by Herodotus,
violent men in unplanned graves.

The other drowns in sickness of rain.
His story always comes back to rain,
its feel like fingers on his face,
its chill like nostalgia
for the woman he'd loved
who murdered him twice when
she brought him back to life.

"Are Your Emotions More or Less Intense?"

—rehab workbook

I went to a psychic, & she told me I have an old soul,
says the Starbucks barista who resembles Cameron
Diaz, who'll never be an old soul because she's caught on film,

childlike. I want to reply with a trite line,
but what comes out is *Thanks for the latte*,
my thoughts too cluttered for quantum entanglements &

small talk. At eight, I was old, my eyes calculating
trajectories of escape, scanning my slightly
feminine watch to figure out how long I had to wait.

My brain made other plans rather than commit
to now. Mind-weary, head-worn, terrified—
back then. Emotions stop aging for an addict,

according to the texts, as long as drugs
maintain their grip: if true, I'm in my twenties—
anxious, desperate for attention, happy for strange words

from the woman who makes hot drinks, despite
how I answer: hesitant, uncertain, my hand reaching
for the steel grip of the door more than half a room away.

"Is Not That Which Is Loved in Some State Either of Becoming or Suffering?"

—Socrates in Plato's *Euthyphro*

my friends worry they are bad parents
broken in bed
invisible to men
who loved the women they were
in a dream
my friends cannot sing anymore
because of cancer
careers
unhappy marriages
they have not played their drums
since the last millennium
my friends
carry their boyfriends to the creek
from a stone footbridge
throw them in
vicarious as glass pebbles
symbolic gestures
my friends move to faraway cities
wish they were here
or I there
wish the scrapers didn't reach the sky
wish the moon were brighter
rivers wider locally
my friends are my friends &
can't know
how I collect their bruises in a jar
map the scars on their psyche
trace a finger
along their slit wrists
awkward tan lines
palest skin beneath their wedding bands

"Are You Worried About a Breakdown?"

—roadside billboard

I have bad spots like bruises in an apple's meat.
Maybe the whole tree's rotten to its roots.
Tensions build. Anxiety thrums
its tuning fork inside me.
Then comes Stress, Strain, &
Worry. I tell myself: *I won't
get my news from Facebook, I won't
get my news from talking chimps*,
but I have this banana handy.

What if I snap? It's not like I'm Rambo
taking out some Viet Cong squad.

Last week, I started this exercise routine
to calm me, help me
control my blood pressure, weight,
hope for the future. Today,
I'm suing myself for intentional
infliction of emotional distress.

There's too much human
in being human, & not enough
being. All I want. I'm that guy
who thinks the Serenity Prayer's too long.

"Does That Mean You Really Want Me to Have a Terrible Day?"

—Marne Wilson

A terrible day's the one we won't see coming.
It doesn't slap us around; it silences
shrill cries of those finding us absent
from our tender boxes.

Happy or unhappy days
are all a man can bless or curse us with,
null days more likely as we sit,
numbed by space between our eyes &

the TV. Maybe we'll smell grilled cheese
sizzling in a nearby kitchen,
then perk up, though hunger waits
for us to fade our moods.

Next, a doe dashes through the yard,
trailed by two fawns speckled like
photonegatives of still-life
with chocolate-chip cookies.

That's what I wish for you, friend:
a three-deer day with grilled cheese &
baked goods, even if that was
yesterday, the same again tomorrow.

It means the terrible never found you:
you scuffed your bike but survived your
Snake River Canyon jump, felt energized
with thrill, even if you broke a bone or two.

"Do You Think of Yourself as a Winner?"
—religious leaflet

I put my law degree to use
in prison,
which must have made
my old professors proud.
They gave me
something valuable,
unquantifiable;
I earned a few
parentheticals &
footnotes of release:
leaving my steel bunk behind
like a hermit crab's
improvised Coke-can shell,
trading it for a room
with books,
hinting at technology.
I listened
to hard men—
angry, almost crying—
explaining their problems
with affection
one might have
for a third arm
or vestigial tail.
I knew the answers,
could see the future
as if on a movie screen
watching the hero
die again & again.

"What Makes You Happy?"

>   —Facebook info box

Talk, please. My anxieties
from childhood left me
weak at speaking. Tell me
love, death, & bruises.
Share your broken marriages,
nights like a singularity
swallowing suns
you spent in motels
no one knows by name.
Small to big, weather
to the weight of being—
give me more: whispers
around laughter, whatever's
said in sleep tongue.
I'm insatiable for conversation
when I have none
like the sex addict who can't get off,
dope fiend who can't recall
why he ever loved the feel
of dying—*it's touching God*,
he says, *then pulling back*:
how I'd describe this
dialogue across a table
at some dimly lit café
in a city many miles
from where we are.

II.

II

"Who Am I That I Am Not on Trial or in Prison?"

—Walt Whitman, "You Felons on Trial in Courts"

Think of those films that begin as the ex-con exits
through extended, shrieking gates—hesitant, squinting.

You expect his struggle. Crime works into his life
however he tries to avoid it, bloodshed's omnipresence.

Do you want him to succeed? Not much of a movie:
parody in dullness where you sought entertainment.

Is it possible to relearn innocence? Shadows tempt you.
The courtroom awaits like gallows built

before you were born in anticipation of you.
Those icy chains? Though you refuse to put them on,

they clank on the hook where they've been hanging.
Listen as the jangle shrieks. You'd like to be

the hero once, but it's you who walked through gates,
afraid, as though you've been on trial all your life.

"So What Is the Line Between Memory and Hallucination?"

—William S. Burroughs, *The Adding Machine*

We were in love; we weren't in love.
Our bodies focused a frequency channeling the Divine.
How ugly we were, & how beautiful, man
over woman, & woman man. Our nights
lit up with candles, jacks-o-lantern,
overhead lamps cleansing the darkening pain.
She came in a wilting anger; I held back with ecstasy.
It was the beast of times, the washed of times,
scented in orange blossoms, jasmine, & vanilla.
Hands read the braille on her skin,
lips drew blood from a turnip. We were
in love; we weren't. Our eyes never saw &
never see the truth, a phantom limb
recalled like a novel read in youth.

"Isn't It Gravity That Ultimately Gives the Grave Its Gravitas?"

—Ron Houchin, Facebook post

To say of those assembled that their faces turn down,
forced by nearness to Earth, its mass in space, &
what keeps them hanging on when they'd prefer floating
into emptiness: it's an answer, though to questions
with their own weight. Another effect: a sinkhole,
minor indentation, formed at the headstone
of my stepfather's grave. Mom obsesses over it
like a second death, not so sad as angry
that she can't be sad to perfection because this glitch
replaces one discomfort with another. Gravity
did this, or careless groundskeepers, backhoes
stuffing insufficient dirt into the pucker.
I prefer gravity of the scene in *Hamlet*
where two clowns dig up the jester's skull—
both mocking & frivolous, happy with their lot,
until a rich man comes along, takes their parcel
as a prop for lecturing the next rich man
on his philosophy & whatever is & isn't there.

"If I Came in Here Shot, Would You Say I Had a Lead Problem?"

—John Van Kirk, *Song for Chance*

I'd say you had an America problem—
wrong place, wrong situation.

I'd say you could use a good drug problem
or never-ending cup of whiskey,
good stuff first, cheapest ever after.

I'd say you've sprung a leak,
might need a cork, or rubber cement.

I'd say I can't stand the sight of blood,
the site of blood, the cited blood.

I'd say have a seat, *friend*,
while we wait for the wound to pass—
as if any of our pretty eruptions
leave the petty party memory is.

Don't know bullet holes, but
I have punctured & been jabbed.
I've walked face-first into a fist.

Who hasn't had his nostril opened
like a box-wine tap; eye
purpled, yellowed in the healing;
tasted rust-mouth or the salty underlip?

Don't come in here shot if you can help it.
If you can't, I'd say you had
a weakness where stability should be,
especially at your age, even at mine.

I'd say you had an insurance problem.
I'd offer to pick up the check,
but it's not my turn.

"What Is Your Idle Job?"
—mass email's subject line with typo

I wait for lunchtime at my desk, spinning
like a boy in a barber's chair. Come noon, a walk
past pretty girls in flowered clothing, faces blooming
from sunlight's brownish blush. I sit awhile,

lotus-like beneath a shady willow, breathe smells
of cut grass, melting chocolate.
I feed squirrels, sing love songs to pigeons,
watching as they bob their heads in rhythm.

Then it's back to the office for coffee
tasting like gasoline, maybe a doughnut on the sly.
If my boss pops over, checking my progress,
I greet him with a good-natured pat on the back
to wipe sticky glaze from my fingertips. After,

it's time for all the important tasks: I shuffle
blank pages, transfer calls to disconnected numbers.
I wink at my window-reflection. I liaise. Mostly,

I deal with people who come looking for me.
I give directions, always surprised if they re-
appear, winded & flushed, to ask me where I am.

"Can Cockroaches Die of a Broken Heart?"

—Randi Ward

for love of nest & undersink,
love of a breadcrumb just beyond the boot;
for love of darkness—a love
like many that fails in golden rays;
for love of rotting-celery stench;
for love of moisture—might one
call that love when drowning in it?
would you be offended if I said
they are like us, but with diverse lusts &
expectations? their abdomens
conceal a majestic organ
that will shatter in the scattering
as ours must when, say, one
flees south to safety while the other
lingers, lost in ornamentation
of someone else's favorite holidays.
it is a form of suffering, isn't it?
we don't die from it,
but scurry under a door
or up a wall to freedom.

"Would You Be Willing to Bail Me Out?"

—Ho Lin

Have you earned steel doors, cinderblock walls,
the squat-&-cough, delousing? I did &
would forgive any man with pennies to buy his way free.

Help if I could; I'm still paying for my last pretty wounds.
Once you're in, you're never really out again,
a dance that doesn't leave your feet when you lean,

sit, or sleep. What did you do?
What do any of us? Tell me
you're innocent, & I promise I'll believe you.

It won't matter once that music starts,
your prosecutor hums a tune, the judge teaches
how to play the blues for beginners.

"Then Why Am I Made with Such Desires?"

—Dostoevsky, *Notes from the Underground*

For years my fantasy was all would return to normal:
my house with its odd angles,
my work desk in the room of orchid walls.
Again, to wake from dark into dark,
to stumble from bed & along that long gauntlet of cats
toward the ten-dollar coffee maker—
I wanted to craft a future from the past,
something so like it as to bookend suffering.
I dreamt about escaping up that shadow hill,
down the steep drive & past the lady crab apple to my home
where I hid myself under layers of leaves
in the overgrown garden. Even as I slept,
I knew armored soldiers came
to reclaim my body from the earth.
I had walked through my front door
a time too many. Homeless, exposed,
what I desired was what I had lost &
never really wanted until then.

"What Have You Lost?"

—rehab workbook

sensation of rain on skin
the moon-eye

walks along the Ohio
at 2 a.m.

how a body feels
its humidity

its badger hands slowly
burrowing holes between my ribs

what meat tastes like
off the grill

a little privacy
please

jokes shared
with anyone

not gathering dust
in a cage beside me

*

I stepped too lightly
on the Earth

fell off
I drifted

through life-space
like a missile

made by mistake

from a dropped bolt

I lost my footing
lost my place

    *

my eyes learned
to love a wall &

cracked jaundice
of the upper bunk

    *

I breathed scents
of men like mud &

woodsmoke
like a sewer

I slept & dreamt I was free
I lost that too

    *

the house
the car

their broken pipes &
faulty parts

the overgrown lawn
flooded basement

mortgage bills & fees
I want them back

what I gave
to rid them of my life

"Have You Ever Loved Someone and Still Felt Lonely?"

—Jennifer Hall-Farley

Sitting hunched on a stone bench,
lulling in dark, surrounded by it &
crickets hopping on their unoiled pogo sticks,
I have my cigarette, &
I have the harvest moon—
a flash in the sky like staring
into the barrel of a pistol as it fires.
Smoke chokes me, invites me to awaken.
The moon has a face,
but I stare at it & see colon-
asterisk-semicolon.
The moon knows punctuation.
The moon knows less about endings,
dragging on in its detachment.
I was like that once: hoping
for a kind word, a hand to hold,
a memory making itself from dust.
My sighs could fill the pages of a novel.

"What Will You Do If You Hit the Jackpot?"

—spam email

I have shackles to break instead of rocks.
For an ex-con imprisoned by his past,

no more withering under steamy glares
of job applications & government-

healthcare questionnaires; no worrying
about the cost of dental extractions,

my car's next part that breaks & needs replaced.
Cash on wood, as inmates say when they mean

six bags of chips for a cigarette,
ten candy bars each for contraband CDs.

I want a free man's money so I can call myself a free man,
too—my shoes as shiny as iPhone screens,

suits steely sharp as scalpels, pillows
soft like plastic sacks of slightly stale marshmallows.

Registers will praise my name
when I buy my way out of this jam I'm in,

dazzling with glitz & bling
like a silver skeleton key on a silver chain:

it opens gates—not those which confined me;
those I carry with me where I go.

"It's a Sexual Song, Isn't It, That Crickets Sing?"

—Stephen Dunn, "A Petty Thing"

You know the tune of the moon band,
harmonies meant for kazoo & tambourine.
Sounds like a jet-engine clock.
Its alarm strikes midnight first,
then noon. It says, *I want you, baby.*
Want me, too? I'd squawk more
if you let me, but you've closed the curtain,
stretched a towel at the base of the door.
I'm too old to keep a whistle like that
in my pocket, thrust with my little guitar.
Doesn't this rhythm arouse your interest?
Knowing soon we might be snatched
by long tongue or bent, calloused talon?
It's a song of endings: dirge. Come,
play it with me as the last leaf falls &
quietly, quietly mourns the loving ground.

"Did You Ever Switch from One Drug to Another?"

—rehab workbook

The straw knows no master.
It worships at its favored temple,
strays toward momentary cults
of joy. I dabbled. Chased the high,
the dragon. Chased security.
Chaste because I lost a step.
I'm not a proud man often enough to matter.
I remember crawling over carpet,
feeling for fragments of pills that flew
in the crushing. Sometimes I found them;
others, rocks—how could I tell
until one nostril smelled the ancient corpse,
membranes burning like matchheads?
I tried to snort the Earth in one long line.

"How Do I Get a Signed Copy?"

—Jeff Santosuosso

I love the sound of that, & the being asked,
how a young model, thin as an icy wind,
must feel when confronted with her initial glossy.
Like the spy's friend in a novel,
the getaway driver, I want to shout,
"Here! This way! I have your escape
route mapped out with the GPS."
I'm a man who signs things: books,
credit-card receipts, confessions.
I'm a man who struggles to reach the station
although his bus already pulled away.
That's how it's seemed each time
I've waited for the next to come
for years. For you—friend, reader—
I want to put my pen to paper.
I'll laugh aloud as though it's meaningless,
while I pinken as I pause
to thank myself for my successes.
I'm like an obnoxious wedding guest
who, after a bit too much to drink,
invites the bride to dance,
expecting he can have anything,
although his clumsy feet must never lead.

"Would Any of Your Friends Enjoy Adultery?"

—Goodreads post-review popup box

Something to be said for unfamiliar hands,
lips angled along a different path,
scents not like the Irish Spring,
lavender oil, or vanilla you recognize
coming from another room.
Would you seek the knowledge of it
like falling through a thousand sublinks
starting from one on a Wikipedia page
about Lord Byron, say, or Gary Kasparov?
I imagine the hope feels better than the orgasm.
I imagine new sounds of laughter.
Yesterday, I posted this question on Facebook
after it flashed unexpectedly like flirtation,
but my friends, I suspect, were afraid to click *Like*
lest someone think they wanted more.
Maybe in their quiet neighborhoods,
their houses had no doors; just
porch steps & welcome mats,
Van Morrison crooning from a stereo upstairs,
his voice reaching sidewalks, streets, &
passersby who stare down at their feet.

"Shall I Send You Some Bitter Broth?"

—Randi Ward

Let the soup stone salt my swollen lips.
Let each noodle slither down my throat.
I like it better bitter than the customary
Hope you soon recover. Call me
over cans & string to tell me
Get yourself together.
How I welcome your miserable salute:
thumb in my eye—cursing, coughing.
Who needs tenderness at times like this?
I'd rather spend these hours on remorse.
Give me the slap-bass sing-along
with grief. Teach me to feel
the groove amidst my funk.
I'm sick, not sainted, martyred,
meritorious. That bleak batch
of stew will do. Warm me
with malice if you'll first allow me
little brittle crackers of repose.

"But What Are You Celebrating?"

—David Lehman, "April 10"

I'm an unemployed ex-con hiding in a red state,
which sounds like the character sketch

for the protagonist in a disaster novel
in which I'm on the run from someone,

chasing someone else—I don't know,
haven't read it. If I'm living out a thriller,

it has a dull middle I can't get past
like when I first took on *The Divine Comedy* &

gave up halfway through purgatory,
never finding my way to paradise.

If I'm celebrating anything, it's that my life
has slowed to a point where horrors don't haunt

or holies entice. Can one go on a quest
without moving? I seek the Grail in stillness.

I savor how I might close my eyes, wake up, &
not see prison bars. What a party:

it's happening now, again tomorrow.
I look out my window but don't fear cops

wielding blue flames & billy clubs.
A joyous occasion. You should try it.

I extend an invitation, though you have to
pass through hell on your way here.

"Do You Like Yourself?"

—religious pamphlet

No one believes me when I say I'm happy.
Nobody thinks a man could write so much
about his suffering, pain, & loss, &
not blink out of the universe
away from whatever paradise a moment is.
Around me: death, regret, divorce,
plus memories of shock & awe,
the TV's glittering dust of tower-fall,
twice over. I spent so much time
crossing the yellow stone of prison floors
that I learned to sing as I skipped above them.
I waved the brightest flares in a shadowy room.
Even now, I'm smiling, giddy.
Clumsy fingers squeeze their ache
into my pen. I'm happiest then,
like a dog that doesn't know its master's dead.

"Isn't Today Worth Fighting For?"

—found scribbled in an old journal

I don't know what I meant
on a different today than today's use of same
back before the turn of the millennium,
before drug problems, rehab, & jail,
before divorce—a time before questions

mattered to me, or the answers
I find inside me as if scrolls.

I can't say if I intended to respond,
if the words were someone else's
left too long in a notebook in a drawer.

It's my handwriting, I'm sure:
squiggles & stains of a black snake
slaughtered on the road by an 18-wheeler.

Not my sort of sentiment. Not then.
There's too much hope. I wouldn't
promise myself the excitement
I feel in today's today as I watch
chipmunks disappear down invisible holes,

a crimson woody climb an oak
when it could fly more easily,

or on TV, TBS showing old movies
that remind me of my childhood—
a time when I still thought life
would be all starships & laser beams.

I wasn't dreading it like the 1990s' me,
the one that must have written this line
I find so surprising I had to
prove it wrong to learn it's right.

"Why Are There So Many Starlings, Darling?"

—Diana Aliff

Winter arrives for all of us, &
ours is not the long grass
but safety of the under-roof.

We are like them
in our need to mass & huddle,
sing, squawk, & curse

power lines that run through our existence
like maps of discord,
a GPS to conflict.

Gray skies make crows of all
winged clusters, but look closer:
starlings carry the cosmos

on their bodies, eyes of thieves
staring backward to infinity.
Because winter, of winter, is winter.

They gather for the wake
of a warm friend, &
we stand near them on their angry ground.

They must remove themselves
from winter, as we must
uncover our sweaters

smelling of dust & closets,
close the book we've been reading
about how calming autumn is

with its colors & rain,
such rain, the rain
that doesn't seem to end until it does.

"Where Do You Go Between Breaths?"

—Donna Wojcik

I've filled a concert hall with caesural pauses,
waited for applause to move through exhalation
to the next performance. I love the music
of what's between one state of being & the next.
It keeps me leaning forward,
building crescendos that never seem to come
until they do, & my body releases,
eyes blink away the past like a rotten memory.
Whatever throated a moan before meant nothing:
false idols, other breaths with their magic flush
that paled long ago. I enter this auditorium
where a crowd of sighs demands attention.
I attempt my melody of absence.
On the score, we mark this as a rest.
In the orchestra, the tension builds at last.

"Do You Think It'll Be Okay?"

—Grace Welch

City truck backed to the curb—
its industrial pipe inhales leaves.
The hum it makes: dentist's grinder
finding a nerve, muffled cries behind.

I watch exhaust fumes bedazzle sunlight,
forcing their will on blur & shimmer.

Behind that veil, a thin man in luminescent vest
directs the tube, cleansing corners,
deleting piles. Such debris. I read somewhere

ten years after humankind's collapse,
the world will have returned to nature,
building new-growth forests
out of concert halls (now silent) &
churches (Word no longer spoken here).

Squatters on borrowed land,
we fight to hold on to property
we think we own. We block traffic.
We make a joyful noise.

III.

"Couldn't I Tell Them Other Truths?"

—Stephen Dunn, "What They Wanted"

Did you hear the one about the dwarf
who stumbled into the AA clubhouse like a frat boy
after an afternoon of drunken volleyball,
dropped onto a chair, then dripped from it,
spilling himself, unconscious, to the floor?

Not a joke, it's a story, & like many stories,
it involves a pint of vodka propped atop the sober table.
Ex-lushes—read their expressions—
debated their sudden hunger over whether to save
the bottle or the man. Which path braved disaster best?

Someone phoned for an ambulance, &
someone latched onto Popov's red label,
emptied potato wine into the sink.
Moments though, you could see
eyes praising & damning gods

of small men—not small like the dwarf,
one more customer waiting in line
at the all-hours marketplace,
but small like themselves as they once were
before they came to on floors of their own,

brushed their boozy tongues,
sought help & hard-made amends
for whatever monstrous things they might have done.

"What Syllable Do I Chant for God to Hear Me, and at What Frequency?"

—Karen Craigo

It plays in B-flat, the same resonating, omnipresent,
from radiators, power lines, low thrum of machinery.
How it throats its solo sutra, *sotto voce*, always
though we've tuned it out, absolving our ears of its static
like an echo left from the Big Bang: not Zen *Om*,
but *Oh* of a sigh—pleasant release, fracture of self.
It moans in harmony with us to recognize
our hard luck, stubbed toes, existential doubts.
It sings along to sudden hymns of gratitude
when good news or friends arrive.
Oh, we whisper, squinting, as confusion handcuffs us
or a hiccup catches us unguarded. *Oh*,
we bellow at the brightening of enlightenment.
Buber preferred to speak *Thou* because
in that word we address the god in us,
god in one another, god in God, but no,
it's *Oh*, the simplest & most common.
It comes, precedes *Lord* in pleading,
yes in ecstasy. *Oh*, we mutter when we learn
the answer to a question that confounded us.
Oh, we gasp when we don't find out.
We love that universal tone: a lyrical B-flat
conceived at the backs of our tongues,
nearer our hearts than our sexes or brains,
divinity nesting at the B-flat center of being.

"Can You Really Get By on Three Chords and the Truth?"

—Ho Lin

I like to think of the Ramones as the Schopenhauer of punk,
in dirt of the psyche boldly shouting about wanting
to be sedated, sniff some glue, be somebody's boyfriend.
Theirs was the fatalistic music of half-believing,
self-entrenchment of a kind that would've inspired Dostoevsky
to dance or pound his rugged fist in the air. Of course,
Joey Ramone couldn't be called an attractive man,
so perhaps he better fit the bill as Nietzsche,
quick-witted in catchy aphorism. Saying *What we do for love
is beyond good & evil* has the same eviscerating charm
as *Beat on the brat with a baseball bat*. Music, meaning, &
mayhem—our philosophers thrummed power chords &
faced down the abyss. Isn't it fun to explore profundity
of simple songs? Doesn't it leave our lives a little lighter?
We could add the Sex Pistols as punk rock's Sartre,
a cult of personality (which he was, despite turning down
the Nobel Prize to prevent it, fighting fate
like Oedipus really not wanting to murder his father &
sleep with his mother). Picture the band on stage,
strutting through obnoxious, self-indulgent riffs,
professing a powerful faith in nothing at all.

"Don't You Know That Night Is Coming?"

—Adam Zagajewski, "Flags"

I wait for twilight when
a woman asks me for directions
to the mortuary. I tell her where to go,
knowing the way instinctively although
I haven't been there. She thanks me,
smiles thinking of the dead.
I was alive before night ended once,
born awake while others slept.
I must have heard the voiceless all-there-is,
even as an infant found marriage
in that stillness. Now I wait for it,
might never sleep again.
I will listen to music on the car radio,
point eyes toward the moon—
a jeweled martini, electric apple
carrying wisdom behind a rain cloud.
Night comes like a movie
with starting time annulled.
I'm waiting for it as a dream
waits to infect its curious reverie
upon rest. I'm restless,
feeling the urge to move along,
to follow the Ohio to its source
or count the graveyards
between here & home.

"Have You Thought About Your Funeral?"

—Paulo Coelho, *The Zahir*

In place of the minister, silence. God
help me, if a word is said condemning
those who go on living over what they do
to cope with just that unintended fate,
I will singe his fingers with my ghostly flame
while kinetic spirit shreds whatever
book he waves to ticker tape.
I tell you, quiet—after the life I've had,
I deserve it, give it back to all who've paused
to share my passing—but, if you few
muddy travelers come to this isolated pub
agree that peace won't serve as my emcee,
then make it a rock star, 1980s style,
with teased hair to his nipples,
face rouged & lipstick stained,
hands in fingerless Spandex gloves.
Let him cuss & rant like a withered drunk.
Let him praise nothing.
Let him mispronounce my name
right before he breaks into that famous
power ballad, the one that used to
leave girls in the audience swooning &
reaching out to touch his sweat.
Let him grab his crotch & gyrate
as he flicks his tongue at those reporters
who came because they thought
I was somebody now that I'm no one &
comfortable at last inside my skin.

"What Do You Most Want People to Say About You When You're Gone?"

—Janet Reed

He may have missed opportunities—
career advancement, pleasure, the lottery,

etc.—stumbled drunkenly through unlit alleys,
crawled despite no humility required.

He might have cut his scalp
on the moon's blade a time or two too many,

stubbed his toe on his lip.
He must have raced through innocence,

indifference, & rage so fast he couldn't catch
a snapshot with his camera set on rapid shutter.

Yes, he screwed his eyes &
screwed up everything he touched,

from love & lust to poetry,
his mind like shrieking instruments

played by a man who juggles cats,
but at least he got this last thing really right.

"Why Do I Have to Die?"

> —Philip Levine, "My Son and I"

I've just gotten used to the sense of my skin,
consciousness in it whipping a still sea.

A lie. I won't feel right if I live
to a hundred & eighty. Crookedness

never dwindles. I look wrong, too,
in these clothes—baggy flannel & cargo pants,

loose like a plastic grocery satchel
hooked like a flag on thorns of a rosebush.

I want to live, keep going, find meaning
in something, leave something meaningful

behind. That's not to say sickness
has taken me on its long, inelegant carriage ride

or that I expect my enemies to target me.
Tomorrow or in twenty years I might

slip the curb & greet a milk truck face to face.
Second Friday after New Year's, I could

forget myself & lean into an accidental overdose.
In ten seconds, I may fall on my writing pen

as I race upstairs to answer the phone.
Response waits for every question.

I don't want it. No matter the complaining,
I'd prefer to go on being

as if I've won the lottery, lost weight,
learned to dance, embraced all humans left.

"Why Is America So Obsessed with Guns?"

—Ellen McGrath Smith

Eight in the morning, shots poison the moment with their loud accounting. From my mountain, I might not learn the where of them: neighbor's house, woods, dirty streets of the city below. I know the why is love ... for vengeance, target practice, hunting. Maybe the news will tell me later how a man loved murder during a deal gone bad, else officers loved their fear of a child on the corner reaching for his phone. If not that, coming silence on the subject reassures me someone loved how soda cans explode like a stained-glass window shattered by a stone, loved the arterial spray from a buck collapsing earthward like the meteor that someday kills the world.

"Why Don't You Wear a Watch?"

—Grace Welch

Time demands, & I succumb
like an easy mark for backstreet hustlers.
No, I swear, I don't want any,
but there I am again: checking the clock,
counting down to the next ending.
I'm a man who can't wait,
resist a pull against the curtains
out of fear he'll miss the squad cars
creeping like tanks up the narrow road.
Time talks down to me like I'm a child.
I listen, scared of its leather belt,
its blunt-force backhand stroke.
I must break myself of time's bad habits
which are constant as a metronome
(I play along but can't find rhythm).
I never want to check the hour again,
although I do, obsessed as any Ahab
measuring his world by ancient wounds.

"Do You Hear the Wind Rising All Around You?"

—Philip Levine, "Belief"

Remainder of the hurricane
square-rooted out of existence
curving around mountains
south of here. The meteorologist
calls it a *tropical depression*.
I like the sound of that,
two words not belonging together
as though misery has its
cheery region: Tropic
of Depression. I often
feel tropically depressed,
sad in happy places,
adrift in brightest dark.
But the wind, the wind—
it warns like a stern father,
promises the belt of rain will lash.
Tropical downpour,
blustering spill. What does
wind have against any of us?
It forces its way
through narrows & alleys,
piles a cairn of limbs
around the cul-de-sac.

It moans about how,
in its youth, it bashed heads,
threw down, bloodied
knuckles against stump &
frond alike. When did it
turn so old & feeble?
Like us, it curses, limps,
carries its tropical depression
to the grave.

"Moreover, What on the Face of the Earth Could Have the Slightest Value for Me?"

—Sadegh Hedayat, *The Blind Owl*

The pie man scatters extra cheese above the discs of pepperoni
arrayed in constellations over red-sky-at-night.
Is that a stray onion? A mushroom bite? A blight
on canvas as though the artist signed his name
with a pseudonym, or else a scalpel? How fluid his motion,
how fast as if not thinking at all. He slides it
into the industrial oven, easing it off his long-
armed, wooden paddle like a giant spoon.
What comes out: a golden, bubbling ooze
with shadows, settling to hard like a stained-
glass window decorating the cathedral for a god
whom not only nourishes but loves.

"I Want to Be a Minor Poet, but Does That Mean I Have to Be Sad All the Time?"

—Marne Wilson

have you learned to say *woe* & *lament*
in flat tone that sings depression? I have, &
the song lends me happiness—all the songs
cream in coffee. the major key of greatness
trumpets feelings others experience.
a minor poet, then, must feel too much &
share the rests, seven notes of silence in a scale.
what are we that we should be mutely celebrated?
we swish our pens in replicating hands,
drawing a moon & stars (not ours) in words
denser than the constellation Pegasus.
how do we entice strangers to lie back in their driveways,
look up to us, love us, wish upon us? will they
admire & shape us in their nighttime pareidolia?
yes, now go take shape & let me write this down.

"Who Do You Love If Not Yourself?"

—Unitarian leaflet

I could love being inside the body beside me
cool as night, & warm, but never love
the cool being inside the body warm beside me.
I could savor a cup of coffee cooling on the table,
fishlike smell of after-rain, money to match
my emptiness, & how a wafer feels on the tongue:
sans taste, sustenance, & what's beyond the physical.
Not to love myself means loving everyone the same:
not giving a perfect gift bought like wedding bands,
chocolate, dinner at the expensive Italian restaurant.
It's riding alone on a gondola,
a serenade of silence, sending roses
to no such person at this address.
It's to be Zeus in a shower of gold,
Don Giovanni dangling his baubles & bells.
Night fades into endless night, & spiders walk
on lonely webs, devouring their mates
like vivid, pristine snowflakes seen
then melting into absence on the tongue.

"How's Life Out There in the Real World?"

—Savannah Dudley

Haven't robbed or stabbed a man in years.
I'm not on drugs (today).

I eat too much—the hunger hangover
never goes away. I confess

sometimes I buy the Shoney's breakfast bar
because it reminds me of prison food,

except the bacon which is real &
plentiful as joy of a light heart

in the first few god-touched months after release.
You'll see. The Board waits for all of us:

scrutinizing meanness first, then maybe love.
If there's such a thing as happiness,

you will find it before it fades into the second prison.
Years from now, when you realize part of you

stayed in that place, your friends will wish
you'd shut the fuck up about that place;

you can't—you have to feed
the memory like a dog you trained.

"So, When Do You Want to Die?"

—David Ishaya Osu

It will be a Saturday,
yes—no one must
miss work for grieving.

Sometime in the evening
so my last day
wasn't wasted resting.

An old song—one
that's not yet written—plays
on the radio (satellite,
Bluetooth, YouTube)
already calling up nostalgia

for the long-ago
I'm waiting to experience
as I contemplate
this doom prophecy of self

like watching some giddy,
glowing orange kite
sky-dancing, bobbing,

right before it's
shot down by a drone.

"But Won't You Tell Us How to Live?"

—Adam Zagajewski, "Corridor"

Be obnoxious. Be indecent.
Those who can't handle the surface you
won't survive the subtleties beneath.
Be loud when needed, loudest
in laughter, quiet whenever
others are complaining.
Be a saint in the wilderness,
not some lurker hiding in a cave.
Wear your cage like a summer hat
so strangers might observe your plumage
without reaching a hand for you, &
if they do, then bite. Tonight,
answer someone's question
with a pining pseudo-sigh,
then turn away so you appear
to be keeping your secrets
in a locked drawer. Lock the drawer
containing garments too small for you,
smelling of dust & the cigarette
smoke that doesn't fade.
Be deceptive, but not malicious.
Let the *you* of you become a mystery,
invisible hand moving pieces
at peripherals. Allow no witness.
Force all to speculate, believe.
Then disappoint them.
They never understand you.
Now forgive.

Title Index

"Are Your Emotions More or Less Intense?" 28
"Are You Worried About a Breakdown?" 30
"But What Are You Celebrating?" 55
"But Won't You Tell Us How to Live?" 81
"Can Cockroaches Die of a Broken Heart?" 43
"Can You Really Get By on Three Chords and the Truth?" .. 67
"Couldn't I Tell Them Other Truths?" 65
"Could This Be Where I Premiere My Memories?" 20
"Did You Ever Switch from One Drug to Another?" .. 51
"Does That Mean You Really Want Me to Have a Terrible Day?" 31
"Don't You Know That Night Is Coming?" 68
"Do You Have Any Advice for Inmates?" 19
"Do You Hear the Wind Rising All Around You?" ... 74
"Do You Like Yourself?" 56
"Do You Think It'll Be Okay?" 61
"Do You Think of Yourself as a Winner?" 32
"Has It Gotten Easier to Avoid Drugs as You've Gotten Older?" 23

"Have You Ever Loved Someone and Still Felt Lonely?" 48
"Have You Thought About Your Funeral?" 69
"How Do I Get a Signed Copy?" 52
"How's Life Out There in the Real World?" 79
"How Would You Rate Your Wellness?" 21
"If I Came in Here Shot, Would You Say I Had
   a Lead Problem?" 40
"Is Not That Which Is Loved in Some State Either
   of Becoming or Suffering?" 29
"Isn't It Gravity That Ultimately Gives the Grave
   Its Gravitas?" 39
"Isn't Today Worth Fighting For?" 57
"It's a Sexual Song, Isn't It, That Crickets Sing?" 50
"I Want to Be a Minor Poet, but Does That Mean
   I Have to Be Sad All the Time?" 77
"Moreover, What on the Face of the Earth Could Have the
   Slightest Value for Me?" 76
"Prefer Slick, Feverish Grooves Over Funky Backbeats?" 24
"Shall I Send You Some Bitter Broth?" 54
"So What Is the Line Between Memory and Hallucination?" 38
"So, When Do You Want to Die?" 80
"Then Why Am I Made with Such Desires?" 45
"What Do You Most Want People to Say About You When
   You're Gone?" 70
"What Feelings Did You Try to Manage?" 22
"What Have You Lost?" 46
"What Is Your Favorite Movie?" 26
"What Is Your Idle Job?" 42
"What Makes You Happy?" 33
"What Syllable Do I Chant for God to Hear Me, and at What
   Frequency?" 66
"What Will You Do If You Hit the Jackpot?" 49
"Where Do You Go Between Breaths?" 60
"Who Am I That I Am Not on Trial or in Prison?" 37

"Who Do You Love If Not Yourself?" 78
"Why Are There So Many Starlings, Darling?" 58
"Why Do I Have to Die?" 71
"Why Don't You Wear a Watch?" 73
"Why Is America So Obsessed with Guns?" 72
"Would Any of Your Friends Enjoy Adultery?" 53
"Would You Be Willing to Bail Me Out?" 44

First Line Index

A

A terrible day's the one we won't see coming 31
Avoid, yes. To want 23

B

Be obnoxious. Be indecent 81
blessed rock'n'roll R & B funk folk acid jazz 24

C

City truck backed to the curb 61

D

Did you hear the one about the dwarf 65
Don't play Spades with your cellies at two in the morning .. 19

E

Eight in the morning, shots poison the moment 72

F

for love of nest & undersink 43
For years my fantasy was all would return to normal 45

H

Haven't robbed or stabbed a man in years 79
Have you earned steel doors, cinderblock walls 44
have you learned to say *woe & lament* 77
He may have missed opportunities 70

I

I almost blacked out reciting the tomorrow & 22
I could love being inside the body beside me 78
I don't know what I meant 57
I'd say you had an America problem 40
I have bad spots like bruises in an apple's meat 30
I have shackles to break instead of rocks 49
I like to think of the Ramones as the Schopenhauer of punk 67
I lose myself in dialogue 26
I love the sound of that, & the being asked 52
I'm an unemployed ex-con hiding in a red state 55
In place of the minister, silence. God 69
I put my law degree to use 32
It plays in B-flat, the same resonating, omnipresent 66
It will be a Saturday 80
It wouldn't win an Academy or National Book Award 21
I've filled a concert hall with caesural pauses 60
I've just gotten used to the sense of my skin 71
I wait for lunchtime at my desk, spinning 42
I wait for twilight when 68
I went to a psychic, & she told me I have an old soul 28

L

Let the soup stone salt my swollen lips 54

M

my friends worry they are bad parents 29

N

No one believes me when I say I'm happy 56

R
    Remainder of the hurricane 74

S
    sensation of rain on skin 46
    Sitting hunched on a stone bench 48
    Something to be said for unfamiliar hands 53

T
    Talk, please. My anxieties 33
    The end of the year means now I begin 20
    The pie man scatters extra cheese above the discs of
        pepperoni 76
    The straw knows no master 51
    Think of those films that begin as the ex-con exits 37
    Time demands, & I succumb 73
    To say of those assembled that their faces turn down 39

W
    We were in love; we weren't in love 38
    Winter arrives for all of us, & 58

Y
    You know the tune of the moon band 50

About the Author

Ace Boggess is the author of seven previous books of poetry, including *The Prisoners, Escape Envy, Ultra Deep Field*, and *My Pandemic / Gratitude List*; two novels, *States of Mercy* and *A Song Without a Melody*; and the short-story collection *Always One Mistake*. He earned his B.A. from Marshall University and his J.D. from West Virginia University. He serves as senior editor at *The Adirondack Review* and associate editor at *The Evening Street Review*. His writing has appeared in *Michigan Quarterly Review, Indiana Review, Hanging Loose, Harvard Review, J Journal*, and many other journals. His awards include the Robert Bausch Fiction Award and a fellowship from the West Virginia Commission on the Arts. Boggess was locked up for five years in the West Virginia prison system, an experience which has been the basis for much of his writing. He currently resides in Charleston, West Virginia.

www.ingramcontent.com/pod-product-compliance
Lightning Source LLC
Chambersburg PA
CBHW010046090426
42735CB00020B/3410